ODE TO THE DOG...and other poems

David Croad

BookLeaf Publishing

Presentation by *BookLeaf Publishing*

Web: www.bookleafpub.com

E-mail: info@bookleafpub.com

ISBN: 978-93-95890-83-0

First edition 2022

DEDICATION

In loving memory of Stephen James Lane

ACKNOWLEDGEMENT

I would like to thank my mother Audrey Lane, for always being there and fighting my corner.
I would like to thank my sister Gail for all the help and encouragement over the years and for always being there for me.
I would also like to thank my brother Gareth for also helping me and encouraging me and for being there for me.
Thanks also to Mark Barlow for all the help he has given me - and for the beers!
And finally, I would like to thank my dog, Billy, for being there and making me (and others) laugh with his antics. And for inspiration for the title of this book.

PREFACE

I have been writing poems for many years now, though till now they have not been published. I hope you enjoy reading the selection I have included for you n this book.

David

As I Gaze At The Stars

As I gaze at the stars,
A glimmer of light
I know you are there,
Watching over me tonight

As I gaze at the stars,
I realise though your body is gone
You are still here,
Your soul lives on

As I gaze at the stars,
I reminisce about the years gone by
I shed a few tears,
Have a little cry

As I gaze at the stars,
I have hope
As long as you are still here,
I will cope

As I gaze at the stars,
I think of your favourite song
And when I sing it to myself,
I feel strong

As I gaze at the stars,

I think of you
Heaven exists,
I know it's true

As I gaze at the stars,
I give a little smile
With you there,
I know I can go that extra mile

As I gaze at the stars,
When I'm feeling sad
I think of you,
The times we had

As I gaze at the stars,
I don't have a lot to remember you
But nothing can take my memories away,
That much is true

As I gaze at the stars,
There is a face I can see
It's you,
Looking down on me

Used To

I used to think you were the one
But an argument and you were gone
You walked out my life and closed the door
We'd be one again I was sure

I used to see your face in the shadows of my mind
Wished I could rewind
I cried flicking through my cards you had given to me
Knowing, deep down, it wasn't to be

I used to cry myself to sleep at night
But now I'm alright
I wore my scars like a wounded soldier
But now that's over

I used to be a shell
Longing for my former self
Talking to you on the 'phone
Yet feeling so alone

I used to think I'd never move on from you
Though now I know that's not true
My tears have dried

I'm no longer broken inside

I used to give you poems I'd written
I used to be oh so smitten
But now I know
I can finally let you go

Blood And Gore

The blade pierces the skin,
Blood poors from within

One dead, countless more to go
This is murder most horrid you know!

This bullet,
Pierces his head which is adorned with a mullet

Two dead
Many more left before I go to bed

Another does stagger,
For I have stabbed him with the mighty dagger

After a long day, it has come to an end,
Just like the lives of these men

But before I rest, there comes a knock upon the door,
There's cops, ten or more!

In shock I stumbled,
I had been rumbled!

And I thought the bodies had been buried so well
I guess you could tell

Maybe I left a lump in the ground,
Perhaps you could see the mound

"You're going down!"
A copper frowned

Just my luck
Then the directer yelled "CUT!"

Ode To The Dog

Bark! Bark! Barking at the door
The sound of a big dog the postie was sure

As I collected my parcel he laughed aloud
For the noise was from a tiny Jack Russell
standing barking so proud

When he's quiet and in a hush,
He likes to get the bus
Though he won't complain
If it's a train!

If you were to ask,
I would say my dog is a bus enthusiast!
Stopping at the bus stop fills him with delight
He wags his tail furiously when a bus is in sight!

He's always as happy as can be
Whenever he's with me
He may be small but in reality,
He has such a big personality!

Hey Bully

Hey bully acting so tough
But your act is a bluff

You make others feel blue
By picking on those weaker than you

Your violence and name calling
Is simply appalling

You think you're better than everybody
Although your argument is shoddy

You're not such a tough guy
Your whole act is a lie

You've got it all wrong,
Its your victims that are strong!

Just A Cat

When I was a kitten,
I was bad
I drove my owner mad

I was terible,
I was a calamity,
I drove my owner to insanity!

Yet I was always made welcome,
A saucer of milk was always there,
Even though my claws were bare!

Yes I could scratch,
I scratched my owner in the eye,
Made him cry!

Now I am older and wiser,
I act an angel of grace
Till my owner's left the place

For I am still a naughty cat,
I just wait till the owner's gone,
Then I start the carry on!

Hands Of Time

Time is like an hour glass,
Slipping away so fast

The years seem to rush by
Before all too long the end is nigh

Like a sudden blow,
Death comes to those we know

Our loved ones
Are gone

Leaving only memories in their place
Life seems to pass by at such a pace

So savour every minute, hour, day and year
Put aside your fears

And make it your mission
To fulfil your ambition

You're never too old to start anew
For a brand new you!

My First Pet

My first pet was a lop eared rabbit
When he saw my hand, he decided to grab it!

Though I was alright
For he didn't bite

And inspiration came
I decided Nibbles was his name

He lived right up to my teens,
He'd live forever it seemed

But one day day I discovered he'd died
I'm not ashamed to say I cried

Though I know I'll never forget
The day I got my first pet

House On The Island

When I was a teen,
My parents bought a house they hadn't seen

So off we set
Travelling in a caravanet

We travelled a long way
To an island called Rousay

Though the house was small,
I loved it living there, loved it all

Although the house needed repair
I was glad to be there

Each morning, a bus, ferry and coach to school
But I thought it was cool

And each afternoon travelling back again
It may seem like a pain

Although not to me
For I enjoyed the journey you see

I was all smiles
Back when we lived on the Orkney Isles!

Diet

I looked at my tummy
And wished I didn't find chocolate so yummy!

The bathroom scales
Remind me of my fails

When I try to lose weight
Junk food seals my fate

A diet plan is difficult to make
For I'm too fond of cake!

But I've got a solution
Losing weight can be my New Year's resolution

Though here's a confession from me,
I couldn't tell you which year that will be!

Social Club

There's a social club I know
On a Tuesday I go

Mixing with friends
Until the session ends

Raffle, bingo and play your cards right
It's going to be a good night

Though it has to be said,
My bingo shout's loud enough to wake the dead!

I like to socialise at this gaff,
For I always have a laugh

Telling jokes, listening to jokes too
You'll never be blue

So take a seat if there's one free
And on the stage you might find me

Doing my stand up comedy routine
Though the jokes are not always clean!

Canal

In my rubber dinghy rowing down the canal
Taking in the sights and the smell

I look to my left
And see a moorhen nest

Made from sticks,
Mother feeding her chicks

My arms now slacking,
I hear ducks quacking

Going at a slow pace,
For this is no race

I want to ponder and peruse,
Take in the views

So I look towards the bankings on my right
And see a car all blazing and alight!

A discarded shopping trolley and broken TV,
Oh the sights you can see!

Cafe In The Park

There's a blue building sitting near the park
gates
Where a friendly greeting awaits

As you find the seats,
You may find a tub of treats

But they're not for you,
For this is a dog friendly venue

So sometimes you may hear a bark
From the cafe in the park

If you so please,
You can buy a sausage for your four legged
species!

Or you could get yourself a lunch
The prices here don't pack a punch!

For everything is a fair price,
And the staff friendly and nice

So stop for a breather, for a rest
At the cafe that's the best!

Camping

If you can't find me at home don't despair,
For I might be out in the open air

I like to go camping
But none of this fancy glamping

A canvas tent will do for me
I like it simple you see!

Though when I hear the rains lash down,
I look around

And see my tent has puddles on the floor
Rain falls on my head though I'm indoors!

As the rain makes me wet,
I realise a cheap tent wasn't the best bet!

Chestnuts

One fine December evening, Tommy Benz
Had gone out with his friends

Sitting round an open fire drinking beer,
Telling stories of fear

First there was the ghost of Manor Hall,
Where the ghosts like to call

Then there was the ogre of the campsite
Too close to home, this tale gave 'em a fright!

Tommy shivered as if he was cold
But he was just scared of the tales told!

So he got up to leave
But he tripped would you believe!

Awkwardly he stumbled
Then obscenities he mumbled

For the situation was dire,
His chestnuts were roasting on an open fire!

Time Flies

I visited a memorabilia store
Vintage items galore

As this delightful shop I perused
I marvelled at the things people used

On the floor lay two wooden Ewbanks
Though I've got a hoover thanks!

I saw some vintage comics and bought a few
I read them still it's true!

Then I discovered an antique mantel clock
The bargain price was a shock!

So I went into my pocket to grab my pounds
Whilst hearing ticking sounds

"It's a wind up you see,"
The cashier said to me

"No batteries to replace in this,
Just wind it up for time keeping bliss."

When I got it home I put it on top of my coffee
table
After tearing off the price label

Now I began to yawn so I rested on my comfy
chair
I was so tired I'd just sleep there

But all I could hear was 'tick tock',
That blooming clock!

I covered my ears so I didn't have to listen
Though that was an impossible mission

I finally gave up and went to bed
But I could still hear the ticking it has to be said

The ticking of the clock grew louder still
I needed an headache pill!

In the end I grabbed the clock in dispair
And launched it into the air

As it went whizzing by,
I thought "Time certainly does fly!"

Gossip

The neighbours across the way
Had a lot to say

Peering out the window,
To find any gossip of those they know

Jack from number seven
Is having an affair with Mrs Devon

Maria from number ten
Murdered Ken!

Fred and Paula are back from their travels
How quickly gossip unravels!

Somebody famous Vernie is dating,
How fascinating!

But now yawn my sleepy head,
For its time for bed

For I've got a confession for you,
None of it was true

So apologies if I got you hooked,
For I was merely reading a book!

If Cats Ruled The World

If cats could take over the world,
They would demand to be heard

They would want their water replaced with milk,
And their beds lined with silk

They would then sleep in a cardboard box
instead just to annoy you
They would demand their meals at all times too

If they had all the power,
They'd request snacks every hour

They would vote to ban dogs
The power would be the mogs!

But don't ponder this too deep
For cats are more interested in sleep!

Sorry

For so many sorry seems the be impossible to
say
They're happy to have their own way

Acting like they're never wrong
Even though others are singing a different song

It wouldn't be a crime,
To admit they are wrong sometimes

But even when they're in the wrong,
The lies roll off their tongue

They can cause so much friction
Even though what they say is fiction!

There's little truth in what they say,
Caring little about who they betray

The rumour mill going overloaded,
Thanks to the lies they've told

It seems to have become the way,
That sorry is the hardest word to say

www.ingramcontent.com/pod-product-compliance
Lightning Source LLC
Chambersburg PA
CBHW051758130826
49812CB00033B/1195
9789395890830